If I Were a
Movie Star

by Shelly Lyons   illustrated by Ronnie Rooney

Special thanks to our adviser for his expertise:

Terry Flaherty, PhD, Professor of English
Minnesota State University, Mankato

PICTURE WINDOW BOOKS
a capstone imprint

For Owen, my newest little star—SL
To the cute little girl Audrey who already looks like a movie star—RR

Editor: Jill Kalz
Designer: Tracy Davies
Art Director: Nathan Gassman
Production Specialist: Jane Klenk
The illustrations in this book were created with watercolor and colored pencil.

Photo Credit: Shutterstock/Zaichenko Olga, cover, 1, 22–23, 24

Picture Window Books
151 Good Counsel Drive
P.O. Box 669
Mankato, MN 56002-0669
877-845-8392
www.capstonepub.com

Printed in the United States of America in North Mankato, Minnesota.
032010
005740CGF10

 All books published by Picture Window Books are manufactured
with paper containing at least 10 percent post-consumer waste.

Library of Congress Cataloging-in-Publication Data
Lyons, Shelly.
 If I were a movie star / by Shelly Lyons, illustrated by Ronnie Rooney.
   p. cm. — (Dream big!)
 Includes index.
 ISBN 978-1-4048-6162-6 (library binding)
 ISBN 978-1-4048-6398-9 (paperback)
 1. Motion picture actors and actresses—Juvenile literature. I.
Rooney, Ronnie. II. Title.
 PN1998.2.L964 2010
  791.430'28092—dc22
                    2010000895

If I were a movie star, I would be famous.
Everyone would know my name and face.

If I were a movie star, I would act in all kinds of movies. I would pretend to be someone else. I might be a top secret spy, an evil doctor, or a famous rock star.

Some actors have to try out for a part. At an audition, people watch and listen as an actor reads from a script. They decide if the actor is the right person for a role.

If I were a movie star, I would jet to places such as Australia, Asia, and Africa. Sometimes I would stay for months. I would work on a movie set.

A movie set is the place where a movie is filmed. On the set are lights, cameras, sound equipment, dressing rooms, and much more.

If I were a movie star, I would learn my lines.

I would make screwy faces in front of a mirror.

I would study how other people look when they speak.

If I were a movie star, an artist would work magic with my makeup. A hair stylist would sweep up my hair. I would wear a fancy dress and high heels. My costume would make me shine!

If I were a movie star, I would work with a director and other actors. The director would tell me where to stand and when to move. I would work long hours.

If I were a movie star, I would try to make people's lives better. I might visit hospitals. I might help rebuild a city after an earthquake or flood. I might bring food to starving children. My efforts would help raise money for charities.

If I were a movie star, fans would scream for my autograph. I would scribble my name on their T-shirts. I would thank people for going to my movies.

If I were a movie star, I would pull up in a shiny stretch limousine. I would walk the red carpet. I would pose for the paparazzi.

The paparazzi are photographers who take pictures for magazines and newspapers. They often follow famous people, hoping to get snapshots.

If I were a movie star, I would do my best to tell a good story. My characters would make people giggle and sob. I would be proud to be a star!

How do you get to be a Movie Star?

You have to love the spotlight to be a movie star. Start by becoming a part of your community's theater group. In high school, act in as many plays as you can. It's best to go to a college or performing arts school to study drama and acting. You can also study communication and film. After graduating from college, many actors continue their schooling. They get a Master of Fine Arts (MFA) degree.

There are other ways to train as an actor. Actors' workshops are offered in cities around the country. These classes teach people how to be successful actors.

It's also a good idea for actors to find an agent. Agents help actors find work. Many actors start by working in small cities. They work their way up to larger theaters and, one day, TV and movies.

Glossary

audition–a tryout for a part in a movie, play, or other art production

autograph–a person's signature written on a piece of paper or other object

charity–a group that raises money or collects goods to help people in need

director–the person who makes the creative decisions for a production

limousine–a long, fancy car

line–the words an actor speaks

role–an actor's part in a movie or play

script–the written story for a movie, play, or TV show

To Learn More

More Books to Read

Chanda, Justin, ed. *Acting Out: Six One-Act Plays! Six Newbery Stars!* New York: Atheneum Books for Young Readers, 2008.

Jacobs, Paul DuBois, and Jennifer Swender. *Putting on a Play: Drama Activities for Kids.* Salt Lake City: Gibbs Smith, 2005.

Ziefert, Harriet. *Lights on Broadway: A Theatrical Tour from A to Z.* Maplewood, N.J.: Blue Apple Books, 2009.

Internet Sites

FactHound offers a safe, fun way to find Internet sites related to this book. All of the sites on FactHound have been researched by our staff.

Here's all you do:

Visit *www.facthound.com*

FactHound will fetch the best sites for you!

Index

Look for all of the books in the Dream Big! series:

If I Were a Ballerina
If I Were a Cowboy
If I Were a Firefighter
If I Were a Major League Baseball Player
If I Were a Movie Star
If I Were a Veterinarian
If I Were an Astronaut
If I Were the President